How to Draw
DINOSAURS
For Kids

Author Tony R. Smith

Copyright © 2019 by Tony R. Smith. All Rights Reserved. No part of this publication may be reproduced, distributed, or transmitted in any form or by any means, including photocopying, recording, or other electronic or mechanical methods, or by any information storage and retrieval system without the prior written permission of S.S. Publishing, except in the case of very brief quotations embodied in critical reviews and certain other noncommercial uses permitted by copyright law

Example #1 Practice

Example of (Smudge Shading). Smudge Shading will give your drawing a

Example of (Tonal Shading). Tonal Shading will give your drawing a smooth contrast finish.

Example of (Light Smudge Shading). Light Smudge Shading will give your drawing a complete look.

Example of (Hatching Shading). Hatching Shading will help blend your drawing together.

Example #1 Final

Draw/Sketch

Draw/Sketch

Draw/Sketch

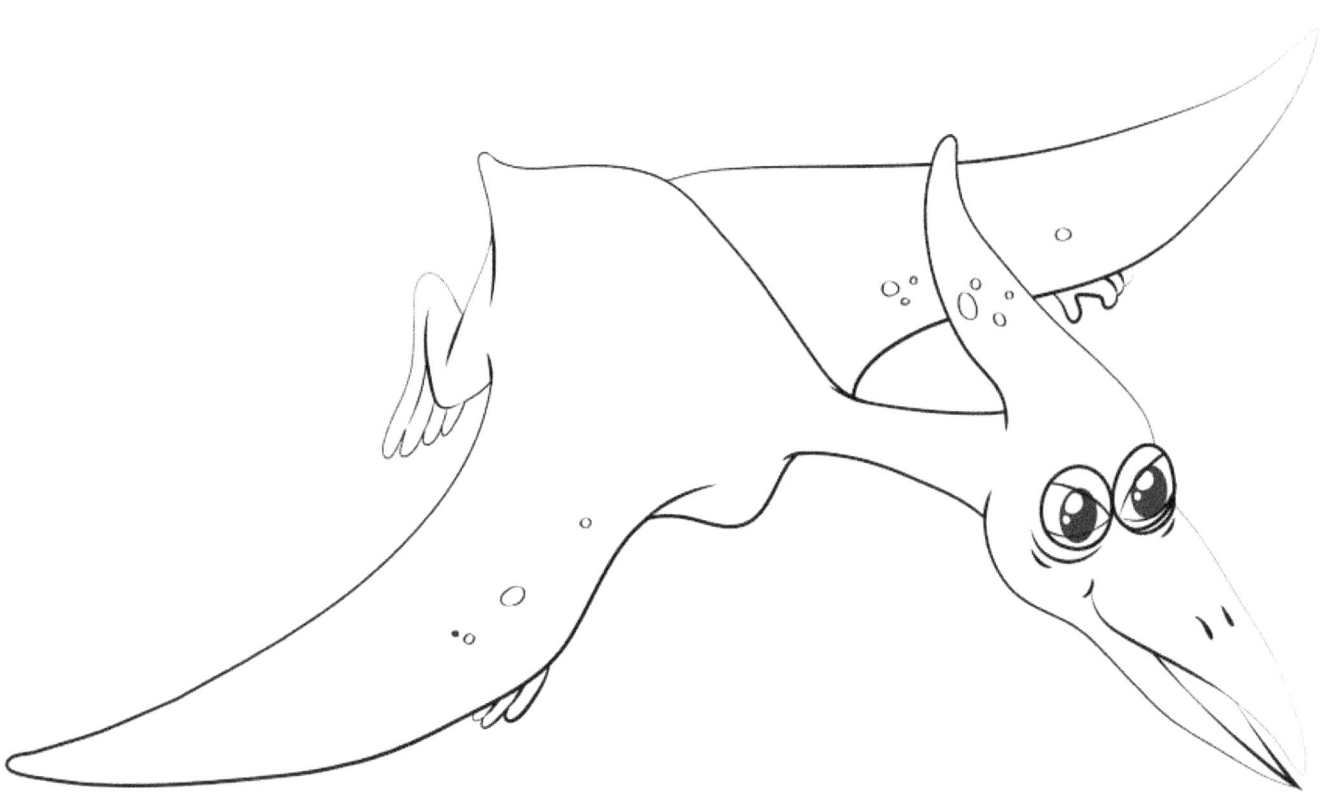

Draw/Sketch

Draw/Sketch

Draw/Sketch

Draw/Sketch

Draw/Sketch

Draw/Sketch

Draw/Sketch

Draw/Sketch

Draw/Sketch

Draw/Sketch

Draw/Sketch

Draw/Sketch

Draw/Sketch

Draw/Sketch

Draw/Sketch

Draw/Sketch

Draw/Sketch

Draw/Sketch

Draw/Sketch

Draw/Sketch

Draw/Sketch

Draw/Sketch

Draw/Sketch

Draw/Sketch

Draw/Sketch

www.ingramcontent.com/pod-product-compliance
Lightning Source LLC
Chambersburg PA
CBHW081733100526
44591CB00016B/2604